Praise for *Unmoored*

"Elizabeth Burk's *Unmoored* pulls the reader into a life lived large and deeply. 'I did float once on the Dead Sea, / my legs straight up in the air,' she attests, a self-described 'aging Snow White kissed/by remorse and an itch for more.' From New York City childhood to Parisian adventures to later-life Louisiana love match, Burk's signature mix of energy, humor, and wisdom urges the reader to 'Suck / the spicy meat and rice mixture from its casing' ('How to Visit Cajun Country'). Unmoored is both existentially serious and massively entertaining."

—SUZANNE CLEARY, author of *Crude Angel*

"As often as I've heard the term 'whirlwind' used to describe a book, you'd think I'd have been caught up in more than a few of those gusts over the years. Truth is, though, I can't remember the last time I've been as swept away by a book of poetry as I was by Elizabeth Burk's new collection, *Unmoored*. These poems whisk us from the Northeast to Europe and back to Louisiana, and they transport us from childhood to gray hair in a breath. Burk's lines are as sharp as any nun's reproaching glance, as rich as any home-cooked meal, and as fluid as fingers hovering over a piano keyboard practicing Chopin. Line by line, Burk puts the knife in our hands to chop onions, she opens a favorite book to its best page and lets us read Marx with her father's eyes, and poem after poem her words pop like a rifle's retort. With writing this exquisite, it's impossible not to be drawn into these poems' memories and blown away."

—JACK B. BEDELL, author of *Against the Woods' Dark Trunks*, Poet Laureate of Louisiana, 2017–2019

"Elizabeth Burk's *Unmoored* invites us to ask of ourselves and of one another—*how did we get so close? / how did we dare?* With sumptuous, precise images and language, these poems ask questions that do not insist on definitive answers, likening the human experience of love, memory and aging to an accident in slow motion. From the searing rooftops of youth to the crisp country house of one's later years, from dripping tomatoes to turtles climbing toward the peak, and from young, boundless love to sustained love which grounds us, in *Unmoored* we find ourselves asking *is there time, is there time?*"

—JOAN KWON GLASS, author of *Night Swim*

"Over the course of an emotionally adventurous life, our heroine moves through landscapes urban, suburban, and wild, but the real journey is a journey of the heart. *Unmoored* reminds us that careful attention to autobiography must include politics, philosophy, biology, spirituality. In one of the book's poised lyrics, Snow White looks in the mirror and asks 'Is that a strand of gray you see? / What does the mirror say, if not that you are not what you seem to be, not what / you think?' Another poem replies: '*Is there time, is there time?*' Elizabeth Burk is fearless and witty enough to turn those questions on herself and demonstrate that after realization comes wisdom, joy, love."

—KATHLEEN OSSIP

"In her delicious poetry collection, *Unmoored,* Liz Burk invites us to join her as she revisits the European coming of age period of her life, explores the world of the enigmatic Louisiana bayou country, and finally awakens to the self-realizing wonder and liberation of impermanence."

And it was all for the fun of it!

... with the waning stretch of life you have left
where you find yourself awakened.
... but your mind remains a spinning top, shining
into dark corners, squinting in bright light'

What will you do?"

—MICHAEL DOUCET, Ph.D., composer/
musician, Cajun lyricist

"Elizabeth Burk's voice rings clear and genuine as she explores the heart and body's deepest rooms. I admire the courage and lyricism the poems in *Unmoored* exhibit while probing the longing and ambivalence of both place and age."

—SHERYL ST. GERMAIN

"In a time when the stories we look to define us, to blast our paths forward with light, are stolen, rearranged and revised without our permission, we desperately need what Liz Burk offers—an indomitable city girl's wily romp through yesterday's good and not so good, the savvy musings of a woman charmed and confounded by the widening world, and a lyrical take on what stays right and what goes wrong as we age. Unmoored, by the way, is no such thing—this unforgettable work is rooted in love, loss, heartbreak, wonder and revelation."

—PATRICIA SMITH, author of *Unshuttered*

Unmoored

Unmoored

Poems

Elizabeth Burk

The Sabine Series in Literature

TRP: THE UNIVERSITY PRESS OF SHSU
HUNTSVILLE, TEXAS 77340

Library of Congress Cataloging-in-Publication Data
Names: Burk, Elizabeth, author.
Title: Unmoored : poems / Elizabeth Burk.
Other titles: Unmoored (Compilation) | Sabine series in literature.
Description: First edition. | Huntsville : TRP: The University Press of
  SHSU, [2024] | Series: The Sabine series in literature
Identifiers: LCCN 2023053761 (print) | LCCN 2023053762 (ebook) | ISBN
  9781680033557 (paperback) | ISBN 9781680033564 (ebook)
Subjects: LCSH: Burk, Elizabeth--Family--Poetry. | Children of
  immigrants--New York (State)--New York--Family--Poetry. | Dual-career
  families--Poetry. | Belonging (Social psychology)--Poetry. | New York
  (N.Y.)--Poetry. | Louisiana--Poetry. | LCGFT: Poetry. | Autobiographical
  poetry.
Classification: LCC PS3602.U7528 U56 2024 (print) | LCC PS3602.U7528
  (ebook) | DDC 811/.6--dc23/eng/20240105
LC record available at https://lccn.loc.gov/2023053761
LC ebook record available at https://lccn.loc.gov/2023053762

FIRST EDITION

Front cover image: Copyright © 2024 Leo Touchet
Author photo by Karen Gershowitz
Cover and Interior design by Maureen Forys, Happenstance Type-O-Rama

Printed and bound in the United States of America

TRP: The University Press of SHSU
Huntsville, Texas 77340
texasreviewpress.org

For Janie
    For Justin
        For Sunflower
            And, as always, for Leo

Contents

III

IV

Many Mysteries

Every now and then a flashback, a memory scant
        as a whisker, a cat brushing against the bedroom door,

a blueberry muffin in one hand, the memory of a man named Stanley
          standing on the porch of a summer cabin in New England,

a woman with long dark frizzy hair, a big toothy smile, another man
               with a straw hat and a guitar and I am on the perimeter

of where I'm not supposed to be. Stanley took me to the movies
        and put his hand up my skirt—no memory of his face, only the hand,

my flowered skirt, the braces on my teeth. Later,
          a hootenanny, a kazoo, circle of folks singing, before the days

of happenings when Charlotte Moorman played her cello topless
              on a riverboat crossing the Hudson and Carolee Schneemann

cavorted naked at an event, her body covered with paint. A surprise visit
        from my old boyfriend, years later. He apologized

for helping Carolee wipe off her body paint in the bathroom, who knows
          what else they did. It bothers him still

that when he returned from the bathroom I had left. Where did I go,
            he wanted to know. I went off hormone therapy recently,

and everyday words immediately slipped into oblivion. I became more irritable
        but that's part of getting old, I tell the man who's my husband now.

He gets the brunt. I did float once on the Dead Sea,
          my legs straight up in the air, by night I traveled over the Negev

on a camel. I've never been to Russia. but I don't regret studying Russian,
> that country spills daily from our lips. *Dosvedanya*, is that hello

or goodbye? Does it matter? What's said one day is reversed the next.
> My parents taped up a map of Soviet Russia, Cyrillic letters danced across

our cracked kitchen walls—Josef Stalin slaughtered for the sake of the revolution
> and Wall Street remains the site of capitalist crimes. What's happened

to the workers of today, my dad would ask, if alive. Inexplicably transfixed
> by orange hair blowing in the wind, Bob Dylan, the revolution,

and an Orange Julius in every working fridge. Many Russians were lost
> after Glasnost—what's this freedom thing, they asked, more salami

on the shelves, American jeans? We want our old lives back. These nights I'm in bed early
> with a laptop, sleeping pills by my side. A night ferry arrives,

picks up passengers stranded on shore, cruises over a starlit lake, sometimes stopping
> at a cabin in the woods where three people stand on a porch.

I

Tar Beach

Growing up in the city
we broiled our bodies on rooftops
of burning black asphalt

turned our fragile flesh slowly
on the spit, dreaming of white sand,
blue waves, bright spots of coral flowers
blooming in tropical sunlight.

Dizzy with heat reflected off
hand-held mirrors, we bathed
in the sauna of our own sweat, fans
of folded newsprint our ocean breeze.

We tied our frizzy hair back with kerchiefs,
picnicked on peanut butter and jelly
sandwiches packed in tin lunchboxes
with warm Pepsis, melting Mallomars.

Evenings in the shower we rinsed off
grime, grit, pinched red blisters blossoming
on pale skin, our heads pounding, nauseous
from too much sun, but still longing

for that tan we saw on TV,
those golden-skinned California dreamin'
honey-blond, silky-straight hair
girls smiling on sailboats,

sipping sparkling elixirs
and waving gaily as their boat
sailed into exotic seas.

Dyckman & Broadway

After school we headed straight
for the candy store on Dyckman
and Broadway where we stood for hours
in front of the comic book racks reading

Tales from the Crypt and *True Romance*
till the sun started down and Louie told us
to go home. Weekends we played stickball
in the narrow streets, a broken broom handle

for a bat, slammed pink Spalding balls
into parked cars and buildings—at the crash
of glass breaking we took off running. Afterwards,
tired, hungry, but reluctant to go home,

we hung out on grimy stoops outside, torn jeans,
skinned knees tucked under chin, watching
the older kids gather under streetlamps,
light up smokes, the girls shoving one another,

jockeying closer to the black-jacketed boys
with hair greased back and switchblades tucked
into back pockets or socks. We savored our last ray
of freedom, the sun glinting laser sharp as it sank

behind sky-high concrete before we gave in
to the waning light, pushed open the heavy
wrought iron door, gateway to our indoor lives.
Cracked marble floors in the lobby, black

wrought iron chairs with frayed red velvet seats,
stained mirrors on either side of the hallway, reflecting.

an infinity of our own images in a hallway reeking
of cooked cabbage, brisket, corned beef.

We climbed endless stairs to the three-room
apartments where our mothers hovered at kitchen.
windows overcooking the potted beef, watching
the kids, waiting for husbands to come home.

At night, when parents slept, we left again
through the window, climbed down the fire escape,
wandered the neighborhood at midnight
soaking up the silent streets we now owned.

The Radio

My mother kneels
                before   the   old   wooden   radio,   turns   the dial,

pokes   a pencil   through broken glass,
                                jiggles the needle—through crackle of static
muffled   words confirm
                a passenger plane   crashed

into a mountain.   *No survivors.*   She kneels, rooted,
                                as if before an altar.
                fists clenched,   gasping.

Outside, skies are dark.
                Rain beats down on shiny asphalt.

Gray curtains embroidered   with cabbage roses
                                hang heavy   with   moisture.
Underfoot   worn gray carpet dank,   mildewed.

She picks up the radio,   hurls it
                at the wall, runs   past me,

through our tiny apartment.
                Heavy metal door slams shut behind her

and I am alone.

My sister and I make room
                for our little cousins   orphans now.

In close quarters   stifled sobs
                heard nightly, sounds   of grown-up grief

the children mustn't hear.

Our Uncle Hershey

He ate rapidly, shiny bald head
bent over the picnic table, hooked nose
almost touching the mashed potatoes
he shoveled into his mouth, oblivious
to wasps buzzing in the rafters overhead.

Behind his back we children giggled.
Where were his manners?
We too had been to camp
for a week each summer
and didn't eat like that!

He talked too fast, tripping over words
as if there were more thoughts in his head
than time to say them, with an accent
that garbled his speech. He had no family
although there had been one before.

A year later he married Edna
who walked with a limp, her hips
rolling unevenly with each step
as if dismounting from a ladder.
She too had been to camp,

lost a family. Neither of them smiled
at the wedding ceremony as they stood
stiffly before the rabbi, she in black
orthopedic shoes, long violet dress,
clutching a bouquet of yellow lilies,

he in light gray, a white carnation
at the lapel. Both of them tensed as
he crushed a glass underfoot, watched

it splinter, then hurriedly embraced
while onlookers breathed a deep sigh.

When visitors came to their home,
he played the violin for them
as he had played for his life at the camp.
His wife accompanied him on the piano.
Always the music got faster

and faster, she struggling
to keep up with him,
he running frenzied towards the end,
trying to capture the music
before someone took it away.

Catechism

From my window six stories above the schoolyard,
nuns with lips straight as rulers, pale eyes glinting
behind steel rims, watched the children at recess.

Priests were equally ominous. Crosses dangled
over large guts, pointing to the place where penises
might be. When the bell rang an eerie silence fell.

The Catholic kids bullied me playing in the streets,
told me I killed Jesus, threatened limbo or even worse,
purgatory. My mother called it nonsense.

I was not reassured. I envied Catholic girls
in their shiny white dresses, ring of flowers
in their hair, young brides, smug in the knowledge

they were forgiven all sins. I, too, wanted
to confess. A playmate led me on a furtive excursion
through massive wooden doors—inside,

overpowering incense, echo of bells and organs,
solemn swish of black robes. A chorus of celestial voices
swelling in unison filled a hollow in my chest—

structure steeped in ritual—compelling, seductive,
it beckoned. *Holy, holy, holy*. I borrowed
rosary beads, learned to chant. *What the hell is this?*

my father barked when he found them
on the bathroom sink tangled up
in his razor and shaving cream.

The Anarchist Colony Goes Republican

I
Early morning, Stelton, New Jersey, gray haired Gusta
      from the chicken farm across the way
         climbs our stairs,

bunioned bare feet, her knobby fingers grasping the banister
      where I sit on the paint-peeling porch
         stroking Sophie, the feral cat.

Across the road two skinny Italian sisters, Jo Ann and Dolores,
      noses dripping, threaten us daily because we're
         Jewish kids from the city and don't believe in Jesus.

We avoid bloodshed with baseball cards. Evenings we capture fireflies
      in jelly jars, pop poison ivy blisters, listen to parents and neighbors
         talk radical politics—the Cold War, unions, Korea.

Jo Ann, Dolores and their parents talk only of Jesus
      and war. Every day they set off firecrackers
         scattering chickens and goats on nearby farms.

II
Years later, my own house in the suburbs sat on an untidy acre—
      junipers raged, tiger lilies grew wild
         on the back lawn. By a steep drop

I put up a fence to keep my baby and my tipsy husband
      from tumbling into the abyss. When we married,
         he resembled a Serbian anarchist—

we marched for peace with gas masks. After the divorce
      I stayed on in the house for years, living with a former
         Episcopal priest, although I still didn't believe

in god. Those days I went barefoot like Gusta, wanted a goat to eat
my grass. Weekends we drove through the Jersey countryside,
found the house of my early summers.

The old schoolhouse down the road—formerly a hotbed
of radical free thought—lay crumbled in weeds,
a chalky heap in this town

renamed Nixon, New Jersey, where Jesus resides
in statuettes on closely shorn lawns,
not a vegetable plot or chicken in sight.

Joseph Stalin and My Father

Give us a child till he's seven and he's ours forever —St. Ignatius

A map of the Soviet Union with thin black Cyrillic glyphs—curlicues
       like dancing musical notes—hung taped to our cracked
         and peeling kitchen walls

in our three-room apartment in the Bronx. Opposite the Formica table
       where we sat for meals, Leningrad,
         Odessa, the Black Sea beckoned.

My father served stuffed cabbage, Hungarian style—
       sauerkraut and onions, preferred sour to the Russian version
         sweetened with raisins. Unsweetened himself,

he admired Stalin, forced to exterminate all enemies, he claimed,
       or the great experiment would surely fail. *Death solves all problems,*
         Stalin said, *no man, no problem.*

Nightly my parents discussed plans to re-visit the Soviet Union,
       bewailing the fate of their favorite tour guide, Max,
         who had been caught having sex

with a Russian male interpreter, both jailed as Enemies of the State.
       My sister and I, silent witnesses at the kitchen table, bolted
         our stringy boiled beef barley soup, ran back

into the streets to play ball until the last ray of sun descended
       behind brick walls, later went on to study Marx
         and Engels, revel in Dostoevsky, Tolstoy, Chekhov.

My First Religious Experience and What I Wore

First time at temple—thirteen and courting
conversion from my family's atheism, I dress

for the occasion in gray circle skirt, peach sweater,
nylons that swish against newly rounded thighs

and my first pair of heels that loudly clack
on parquet floors, despite my attempts

to tiptoe. At the podium a squat bearded rabbi
leads the ritual, quickly leaving me adrift

in guttural sounds of a language I do not understand.
The congregation moves as one, rising up

and down, a tidal movement spurred by cues
I cannot detect. I follow hastily, aware

of my mother's blue and white garter belt under
my skirt, feel the harness around my waist slip lower

each time I stand and sit, feel my nylons wilt
around my thighs. I press my legs together hoping

to stop the descent, but they buckle around my knees,
slide down my shins. The congregation sings on

and for the first time ever, I pray for god's help
to retrieve the silken heap tangled at my ankles

as if I'd been sprinting towards a state of grace
I had yet to learn lies forever out of reach.

Performing Chopin

I
My mother attacks Chopin's
Revolutionary Etude, startling herself
with the stomping and banging of boots
entering Poland. Taking a deep breath
as if preparing to enter a race, she plunges
into the *Minute Waltz*, fingers racing against
an imaginary stopwatch, a race she always loses.

My grandmother jingles her keys, sounds
scraping harsh against music from her piano,
the one she gave lessons on after she left Latvia
for St. Petersburg's Conservatory, then fled Russia,
came to the States. *Now you,* she says motioning me
to the piano bench—I play Chopin's *Prelude in C Minor*,
a piece I will later fumble through at a student recital.

II
Ladies' night in a bar deep in Florida's panhandle,
I meet a woman in a low-cut red dress, dyed yellow hair,
recently returned from visiting Chopin's grave in Paris.
After several apple martinis, we giggle our way
to an old piano in a corner of the bar. She tugs
at her short skirt, arranges herself on the bench.

Her hands hover over the keyboard, then plunge,
a diver, fingers skittering skillfully over Chopin's
Butterfly Etude, the impossibly complex *Fantaisie
Impromptu*. With a silent nod to my mother, I attempt
the crashing chords of *The Revolutionary Etude*. We play
until electronic guitars arrive at midnight.

My Mother's Dreams

It all seems like a dream,
my mother said after my father died,
fifty-five years of marriage, erased.

With those words, we all disappeared,
figments of my mother's reveries.
Her life now a looming blank page,

she met Charles, a Jamaican man
of ambiguous age—white hair, a daughter,
a three-year old grandson, possibly

his son. Charles cooked her lavish
dinners—roast chicken with pineapple,
maraschino cherries, red beans and rice.

Isn't she lovely! he exclaimed
as he wrote himself onto that empty page.
My mother, frail as rice paper, radiant

as never before, awoke to a new life,
wondered which was the dream.
When she was whisked to the hospital

with a mysterious fever, doctors discovered
an infected womb, asked the expected
questions. *Lord, no,* I replied, astonished

at the thought—*my father's been dead
for years.* The doctor paused, let it go—
my mother dreamt on, not waking again.

The Sofa of My Dreams

Once, traveling through the tiny town of Fancy Gap
   in the Blue Ridge mountains of West Virginia,
      I heard a radio announcer say, *and now*

you can have the sofa of your dreams, and I pictured
   local folk luxuriating on sueded slipcovers,
      silken damask over downy cushions,

sipping a cup of tea, a vodka gimlet—to sit
   and sip, perhaps to dream, legs crossed at the ankles
      or spread wide inviting X-rated sex.

My parents' sofa was a parrot yellow print, hard
   as a board, covered in plastic, waiting for company
      that never arrived. My father dozed in his chair

reading Toynbee on ancient civilizations, waking
   only in time to go to bed, while my mother
      filled out report cards at the kitchen table.

There are days the ticking membrane tears
   and what's inside your head, your heart,
      comes spilling out, tick tock, through bone,

muscle, fat. In foamy dreams, the body emptied
   hangs suspended in mid-air
      while the cotton-candy mind floats free,

trying to reach the stars, the moony-sun,
   leaving behind only your feet, grounded
      beyond reproach, on your way to work

or on your way home, where you sink
  into the cushions of your striped couch,
    dreaming of desires long discarded.

Do we expect too much from our furniture?
  too little from our dreams? Will the perfect sofa
    bridge the gap?

II

What Shape Awaits in the Seed of You?

—after David Whyte—

It takes faith to plant a seed
in earth's vast muddy—to dig
a hole, bury it in soil, baptize daily.

Perhaps you'll mark it with a stick
shaped like a cross
while by this mound of dirt

you wait. But what if a storm scatters
your seeds and when the blossoms
burst forth you watch them grow lush,

unruly, when all you wanted
was one flowering stem to place
in a vase by a window where you sit

afternoons sipping tea, a smiling monk
amidst orchids. You didn't plan
for this stranger whose ears wave wild,

whose electrified tendrils swirl
in corkscrew coils, threatening
to creep over varnished deck,

the railing erected to protect. Do you run
for the clippers? Or do you follow
the vines as they surge and spread?

A La Maison de Madame Bellefleur

Our concierge, Madame Bellefleur was constant witness
to a chaotic rotation of roommates, friends, lovers who lived with us
in the huge, three-bedroom elegantly shabby apartment we'd rented
on Avenue Montaigne, across from the Theatre des Champs Elysees.

On the other side of town, in the jazz caves of the Latin Quarter
Jessica picked up men, brought them back to the apartment.
A trail of clothes on the floor—coat, scarf, skirt, sweater,
boots, black tights—led from front door to her bedroom.

In the morning the couple would emerge—bleary, hung over,
stumbling towards the coffee pot in the kitchen where we sat smirking,
the guy eager to retreat after a quick cup of instant, while Jessica
lit a cigarette and sulked. My Spanish boyfriend, who lived in my room

at the end of the corridor would shake his head, cluck his tongue
at us *chicas americanas*, scandalized by our wanton ways. *Pendeja,*
he called her—Spanish for pubic hair, the Spaniards gifted
with colorful curses invoking mother's milk, bodily excretions,

boots, objects not ordinarily strung together in one breath. Secretly,
we called her *clitorissima*. Evenings, Jessica hunkered silently
in our unheated living room, reading *Newsweek*, drinking scotch,
electric heater tucked between her legs.

When MaryAnn got pregnant, Jessica recommended a plane trip
to Morocco, then asking a taxi driver for the nearest clinic.
Next, she suggested crossing the English Channel to seek a doctor
who would declare her unfit. Instead, MaryAnn's lover found

a local doc who inserted sharp objects inside her, sent her home
to call him when she bled. But her cervix closed up like a virgin's.
A week later, all-knowing Madame Bellefleur handed her a slip of paper
with a doctor's name, an address in Rome. *Go,* she said, *before it's too late.*

Il dottore, four fingers deep, thumb rubbing up against clit,
was delighted to practice his English, and his seductive arts
on a young American girl. When MaryAnn returned to Paris,
Madame Bellefleur asked if she enjoyed her holiday in Rome.

Oui, Madame, MaryAnn replied, *although I missed seeing
the Pope—maybe next time.* Madame Bellefleur frowned, replied,
mais non, we must hope there is not a next time.

Phantom Child

He is so like his father—
dark eyes, glossy black hair,
hot-tempered—a Spanish sculptor
whose chiseled arms
forever molded me.

Together we left Parisian nights,
thumbs pointing south,
roamed the student streets of Barcelona,
listened to the blood-pounding rhythms
of flamenco in Madrid,

dined on *paella de mariscos* in Valencia,
lay on tree studded beaches,
ate tuna and black olives from a jar,
swam in the icy Atlantic
and dried ourselves on sun baked rocks.

In Andalucia sweet strains of Malaguena
flowed through the streets,
fragrant flowers tumbled
from window boxes.
We slept in humid *pensiones*
where we conceived the child
I later tore from my womb—

ghost child, grown now,
who inhabits me still,
offers me sangria when I visit
before he turns back, chisel in hand,
to hammer life from stone.

Writing on the Wall

And then you were gone, leaving only a note scrawled
   in red on the bedroom wall, the color of lipstick, mine perhaps,

or another's. I see it still, dripping like the writing that appears
   on a wall in a movie where people refuse to flee the house

that's cursed—they linger, wanting to save their dreams, hoping
   to change the story's end. I did the same.

You fled from the city we roamed together, nights studded
   with neon flickering on Broadway's strip-joint side streets,

the dank, calloused bars where you taught me to drink bourbon neat
   and to discuss Nietzsche whom I had never read, but I did believe

in death rather than god back then, as now—do you see how you
   are with me still, that and your love for words. I read your poems now

and smile. It was summer then, the city in heat, not a breeze between us
   as we wandered up to Harlem for jazz, then down to Max's Kansas City,

you straight out of Kansas yourself but more at home in honky-tonk's
   dark corners, dimly lit juke joints than in moonlit haystacks and the open prairie

that spawned you—lean, lanky, Midwest drawl, did I tell you how my heart
   hurled from my body when I saw you were gone, how I sat in the bathroom

of that rank loft we rented on Rivington listening to junkies on the street
   below, staring at the blood on the wall and waiting for mine to flow?

Who Knows What the Barren Snow Might Bring?

His battered overnight bag, faded brown,
    zipper frayed, burst open as he rushed
to the train to bring him to Poughkeepsie

    where she lived. Underwear spilling out
all over the platform, he missed
        his train. *Cripes*, he said

when he called, whining over his bad luck
    and messy life—a web of deceptions
awaiting disclosure—but wasn't this both his fear

    and his hope? the suitcase chosen to collude
with his unconscious? Her aging unmarried self,
    in a cocoon of anxious illusions, unencumbered

by guilt, had hoped he'd be caught red-handed
    with the candy-colored condoms he'd promised—
would he wear them that night with his wife?

    Forgive me, he said, pleading for another tomorrow.
But the trees were bare and forgiveness
    seemed only a way of wishing for a better past.

Bar Talk

The bartender looks like a left-over prop
    from a Goddard movie—he reminds me
of my Paris boyfriend who dared me to jump
    over puddles. *You're too cautious*, he said. *Get wet.*

A coonhound lies under a table, head between paws, waiting
    for his owner or for the music to begin.
We're all waiting for the music to begin. The band
    hasn't arrived, or they're still drinking at the bar.

I met a former boyfriend in a neighborhood bar—
    I said *restaurant,* he said *bar.*
He lived with me until he left one day without saying why,
    so I packed all my stuff in boxes

and left my home for elsewhere
    in case he decided to come back. Elsewhere
turned out to be another boyfriend
    who drank at home, not in bars.

My father at sixteen waited tables in a restaurant
    in the Catskills when he met my mother.
She was eighteen and waiting tables too.
    He says *restaurant,* she says *bar.*

There are other people at the bar—
    a harsh-looking blond with wispy hair—
she offers her legs as earmuffs for the bartender
    who smiles and shakes his head.

My next boyfriend, a philosophy professor,
    didn't drink or smoke pot. That relationship
didn't last long. The dog's owner returns
    when the music begins.

Come In

Your one-track mind takes the train
all the way to Poughkeepsie

but your philosophical pretensions
won't get you laid—I'm channeling you,

a scary thought, you flood my brain.
I woke up this morning thinking

of James Joyce. As he dictated
Finnegan's Wake someone knocked

at his door. Come in, Joyce said. When
the secretary read back her dictation,

she included those words. Wait a minute,
said Joyce, I didn't say that. Yes you did,

the secretary replied, someone knocked at
the door and you said, come in. Then leave it in,

Joyce said. I think of the night before.
You flood my brain—I leave you in.

Still A Spinster at Twenty-Seven

Whenever I visited my mother
I always brought along a boyfriend
including unlikely prospects
like the bearded jazz-pianist
Hari-Krishna refugee who stood
on his head on her living room floor
to demonstrate his spiritual skills,
dislodging a brass sconce from the wall.

Do you think you'll marry him?
my mother asked hopefully
when she phoned the next day, distressed
over my unmoored/unmarried life of
anti-war demonstrations, women's lib rallies,
astrology charts, dinners of brown rice
and seaweed in my apartment on East 7th
and Avenue D, listening to junkies
shoot up in the hallway bathroom.

Guilt prevailed—I married the next seemingly
stable man I met. Following a ceremony
in the county courthouse witnessed
by strangers, we drove to Rehoboth Beach,
opened a bottle of Jack, called my mother.
My husband assured her he wore shoes—
as if she cared, her daughter was married
to a doctor, every mother's dream,

Soon my husband grew a ponytail, read
Don Carlos, delivered babies in teepees
in the communes we visited, taking on
my hippie ways while I went to grad school
and struggled from bell-shaped curve
through dissertation.

Who could have predicted the avalanche
of empty bottles in the basement, the beached whale
on the staircase at noon while my two-year old
howled from his playpen, the 2am phone calls
to relatives in Kansas, the be-bopping bi-polar
alcoholic roller coaster life with the doctor became,
making my former unwed world look like a stroll
through the boneyard of normal.

Bloodlines

My husband's grandpa, 84, shot grandma
in the back with a .22 while she stood at the kitchen sink
washing dishes, her slippered feet planted sturdy
as if rooted to the worn linoleum floor. He missed.
Although he wasn't drinking at the time, with all that palsy
he couldn't shoot straight and grandma, 64 and in shock,
landed at the local doc's, fifty years of dishes behind her.

When the call came, we were doing rounds,
not shots, on the third floor of Bullfinch, the hospital
where we were young and trying to save lives,
while grandpa was aiming to be the best shot
in West Des Moines. As the story goes,

he thought Grandma Rose was having an affair
with Hannah up the road. They took him straightaway
to the state institution where he died two weeks later,
refusing to live a locked-up life.

At the funeral the family huddled dry-eyed
in the cold, muddy wet, afterwards gathered at
Uncle George's. Grandma Rose, fresh from the hospital
in faded housedress, her wide Serbian face vacant

as the chamber of that .22, told stories of life
with the old man when he worked as a bodyguard
to a Serbian gambler on a Mississippi riverboat,
broke a man's fingers, lost two himself,
before he threw the man overboard.

Were we gambling too when we gave our son
the old man's name—that middle name, lodged there
like a bullet—a name grandpa changed
from Dushan to Thomas in praise
of American ways and the wild Midwest.

Internship—Pittsburgh, 1979

I worked the suicide hotline
      for a six-month stint. Time
stretched, a rubber band pulled
      between wrists. Mine were not yet
cut or mutilated, my legs were still
      un-scarred by scrapes or burns. Up
and down my arms veins popped,
      inviting scissors, knives
and razors like the ones I held
      for my clinic patient far away
from her nightstand. I left
      the blades in my office until she
or I needed them next.
      I was undone by tasks—diapers,
dishes, a dissertation I couldn't write,
      a husband drinking night and day. Often
I thought about calling myself on that hotline
      but didn't have time to make the call
nor energy to answer the phone when it rang,
      nor would I have known what to say
to the person I was running from
      at the end of the line.

Married To My House

My first house in the country—
I fell in love with ancient stone walls,
an abundance of leafy trees,
the slope of lawn and waterfall.

In early years I lingered barefoot
on a wooden stoop in the back yard
savoring spiky green grass between my toes,
planning my garden—hollyhocks, azaleas,
a border of perky impatiens.

Sometimes I wonder
if I loved my house more
than the husbands and lovers who came
and went. The children always stayed—
their stuffed animals and games
crowd my closets still,

while I was wedded
to my country home,
curved dormers transformed
into cozy breakfast nooks,
back patio filled with flowering pots,
even the startled deer who ate my shrubs.

We've been thirty years together—
creaky frames grown askew, plumbing
in decline, circuits that short out on overload,
furnaces that groan if required to ignite—
we shudder, constrict in the cold, bones quaking
and rattling—an aging rock 'n' roll duet.

Did we stay too long together, sink
into an abyss of domesticity?

I drive away from the realtor's office,
traitorous in my desire for shiny new fixtures,

empty spaces, gleaming floors,
windows that open and close
with ease, like an adulterous wife
abandoning a faithful spouse, seeking
the last and saddest divorce.

Repetition Compulsion

It doesn't matter who you marry—
one morning you wake up
and there's your father

sitting at the breakfast table
scowling as he spreads blueberry jam
on a slice of toast, or standing

at the stove, stirring oatmeal
and pointing out the untidy stack
of papers on the dining room table,

the lights you left on in the kitchen
overnight. Your eyes water,
you barely recognize the fragile creature

you've become, so you leave
your father for another mate
discover now it's your mother

you've wed, and it's you who complains
about dirty socks by the side of the bed,
newspapers strewn on the living room floor,

you who are angry and overbearing
while your partner wears the sign
saying *Victim*. You hate the carping creature

you've become, decide it's time to try
again, while the chorus of ghosts cackle,
shutting out all other melodies.

III

Meeting Leo

You're a wild ride,
    never tongue-tied
outsourced Louisiana Jones
      landslide
a camera slinging, ring bearing
        upside down, run aground,
try again kind of guy

I was stuck
    stranded mid-stride
absorbing the babble of suburban
      wives, a misfit marooned
with coffee shop brides
        sipping their snowdrop
Eskimo chais

You careened through my life
    in a red pick-up truck
a respite from mini-van streets
      and I hopped aboard
a damsel in heat
        flinging the map
into the back seat

I fell in love with your hands
    like gnarled trees
your triple E feet, roller-blade knees
      your twisted rope shins
your duck gumbo soup
        your heart like a scoop
 of banana cream pie

Now I bring to you
    my crooked toes

my arms like feathers
      my thighs warm toast
my thoughts like buckshot
        spraying words to the air:
how did we get so close?
        how did we dare?

Watching Him Peel an Onion

His hand, calloused, rough, wide
   as a catcher's mitt, hovers

like a bear's paw over the basket,
   scoops out an onion, cradles it.

Blunt fingers gently press
   testing for tenderness

while a thumb rubs upwards
   over the first fragile layer

of skin, stripping it away
   like tissue paper.

With his knife
   he cuts away the rooted ends

and peels back layers
   exposing the moist inside,

then sets it down
   on the cutting board

where it waits
   white and glistening

naked
   as my beating heart.

Making Love with a Southern Boy

Arms, lips, hips, legs
in sleepy motion
put into place, paced
then raced.

At the end
he whispers
one word —
watermelon.

What! I say,
compare me maybe
to a ripe peach,
a plump persimmon,
a tart plum
but a watermelon?

*Didn't you ever
make love with
a southern boy?*
he says,
all sticky sweet
syrupy drawl,

*Honey,
it just means
I'm thirsty.*

The Road Widow

When you are gone
each city you are in
lights up like a neon sign,
beckons like Broadway
dancers and go-go girls.
I see bars, strangers, ex-wives,
imagined worlds
where you loved others
and left, or were left behind.

My body tilts south
where you have gone.
I taste cane sugar,
feel the wilting heat.
I am surrounded
by weepy trees,
gnarled arms reaching out
over sultry swamps
where the murky deep rises
to meet the sky.

Hurricane Lily Wilts to a Category Two Before Striking Land

I didn't know that massive trees
could be toppled by a gust of wind,
a mere breeze down here
in bayou country

where storms are common,
water everywhere a way of life,
and even the dead
are buried above ground.

I'd expected maybe
a few windows lost,
the tinkle of glass,
some roof tiles, leaving

empty spaces overhead,
easy to mend or replace.
I didn't know the roots
of aging willows lie

planted in shallow earth
and reach out, grasping
for solid ground
beneath the water-soaked soil,

that in the wake of this seemingly
minor storm the landscape
would be strewn
with giants, upended,

naked roots clawing the sky.
I didn't know that a man

like you, so entrenched
in your solitary ways,

your branches spread
across the earth,
would fall apart so swiftly
when I left.

Mistaken and Forsaken

Oh what a joy I thought it would be
   to be free of you,
the rough housing rowdy self
    of you, the noisy clattering
stumbling, mumbling,
      yearning of you.

I didn't think I would miss
   your bawdy bad self,
the talking, slamming, jamming
    bubbling buoyancy of you,
the in-your-face parade.
      Do you miss me too?

How could I know my bones would ache
   from the craving of you,
my limbs baffled by the lack of you,
    my heart heavy as a pebble
plopped in a pond, rippling circles
      widening with a want of you.

Oh how I want to dive forever
   into the deep murky river of you,
the lazy lucid lake of you
    to recline in the silly-billy heart of you,
to glue my elbows to yours,
      to be true to you, to be true.

He Visits Me

Home from work, I find him
in the kitchen chopping onions, celery,
dicing peppers. Peeled parboiled tomatoes
sit naked on the cutting board
dripping juice and seeds. I inhale

the aromas of garlic, thyme,
the white wine poured Julia Child style,
one dollop for the stew, one slurp for the cook,
before he spoons into my mouth
a roux rich and redolent with spice.

Come to Louisiana, babe, he says,
putting into my still-open mouth
a plump piece of hot sausage,
my mouth that is always ready for more,
and I'll cook for you forever.

And I want to, I do, I want that hound dog
in the back seat of our pickup, head poking
out the window, ears flapping in the breeze,
chanky-chank music blaring on the radio
as we drive over bumpy back roads to town

but I'm a set-in-stone city girl,
raised by skyscrapers, wary
of wide-open spaces, afraid my life
will be cast adrift, a pirogue
lost in the tall marshy reeds, empty

as the galaxy of wine bottles he leaves
behind on the kitchen floor, where
papery garlic skins lie scattered,
still curled as if around the body
of the clove no longer there.

Living Alone

is easy, no one telling you
what to do or when to do it,

no one questioning why
you're eating M&Ms so early

in the morning or peeling
a potato with your fingernails

instead of a knife, no one
watching you forget to screw

the top back on the coffee maker
or put the glass pot under the spout,

spraying coffee all over the kitchen,
no one asking what's for dinner

as you walk through the door,
no one there to see that living alone

is as easy as landing on the moon
every night, looking to claim your place

on an empty planet with every
tentative weightless step you take.

Deciding To Marry

We sit in the yellow and blue kitchen
you painted three weeks ago when
I put my New York house on the market.

Which is why we are discussing marriage:
not a romantic proposal—a capital gains gambit;
the money could go for cameras and carpentry,

a better use than bombing Iran, we reason,
as we sit at the round wooden table,
the morning sun glinting through the glass door.

It's mid-March. I am warming my hands
on a hot cup of cappuccino you made for me,
sipping sweet foamy milk, the coffee underneath

pungent, bitter. We watch the birds swoop for seed,
the birdhouse a battleground, a tiny swinging stage
where a fierce chickadee holds sway, chases away

blue-jays, sleek catbirds. A squirrel scampers
up the pole in a futile quest for food, only to lose
his balance at the top, slide to the ground.

We laugh as the squirrel limps away—he'll be back.
Next it will be fox, raccoon and the groundhog
who lives under the deck, coming to dine.

Maybe it's this wildlife family
that reminds you of home—
about moving back to Louisiana,

building us a house like Frida Kahlo's,
all orange, blue and yellow sunshine,
an open courtyard in the middle

filled with foliage, a stone bench
where she sat with Diego—
when they were speaking.

I look at the beige walls, a house I've lived in
for thirty years, not really seeing the trees, birds,
squirrels outside until you came along, and I say yes.

How to Visit Cajun Country

Drag your bags out of the air-conditioned airport
   and into the sauna called Louisiana. Let your skin
   drink in the heat and wet. Try not to think

about your hair. Stop first at Poché's in Breaux Bridge
   for a breakfast of café noir, grilled biscuits, boudin. Suck
   the spicy meat and rice mixture from its casing,

go native and add couche-couche, a dish of corn meal mush
   fried in fat. Find any boat landing on the Atchafalaya Basin—
   Angelle's, Whiskey River, Butte La Rose—to tour

the swamp's still waters, your guide telling stories of life
   in the basin midst mosquitoes, muskrats, the eerie calm.
   Mid-day check out local service stations for a plate lunch

of red beans and rice, fried alligator, crawfish étouffée. Grab
   a nap by the Bayou Teche, Spanish moss dripping from live oaks,
      then wend your way south through the tiny towns of Indian Bayou,

Forked Island, Isles des Vaches, letting flat fill your eyes
   for as far as you can see. Stop for a shrimp-burger at Skinney's,
   paddle a pirogue through marshy reeds, gaze up at endless sky,

white clouds shaped by dreams. Cast a lazy line for redfish,
   trout. Evening, drive north to Dupuy's for a dozen oysters,
   a cold beer. Don't be alarmed by the bartender calling you *beb*,

even your grandma's a *babe* down here. For dinner an okra gumbo
   and a catfish po'boy, then stop by a drive-thru for a banana daiquiri
   to go. Follow the sounds of accordion, washboard, fiddle—

frog festivals, crawfish races, cattle festivals, any local fais-do-do
will do. Before midnight allez danser at the Blue Moon Saloon
where strains of *Jolie Blon'* and *Evangeline Waltz* fill the night air,

dancers glide to the weepy wail of Beausoleil's ballads, boogie to
Buckwheat's zydeco blues. Don't leave until you've danced
the two-step with every stray Cajun you can find.

Learning to Love Louisiana

"Where are the mountains?"
I ask, after an hour's drive
through flat-filled landscapes
of sugar cane and rice fields, miles
without trees, unprotected from open sky.

Some call it the prairie—
the name blows wide open
the shut down, frightened spaces
in my heart,

transforms this stripped bare
boggy land into primal frontier—
grand vistas of grassy earth
framed by cloudscapes,

dotted with tin shacks, trailers
huddled like hitchhikers
by the side of the road,

the lackadaisical towns, windows boarded,
looking in daytime as though
they were shut down for the night,

the gray mist's endless drizzle
filling the swamps, marshes, basins
to the brim.

Why not surrender, succumb, languish
at the edge of a rice field, watching
the wind sway the marshy grasses

out here on the prairie,
so close to god,
where there is no place to hide?

Drinking Margaritas and Talking About the Oil Spill

We're sitting at the bar
drinking margaritas
watching them try to cap
the BP oil spill
but the level of flow
and gush remains the same,
oil continually pouring
into the ocean, washing ashore.

Everyone at the bar
is talking politics—wetlands,
corruption, job loss, how
the blowout-preventer failed,
oil spilling over birds,
dead fish washing ashore,
coastal industries destroyed,

while corporations shrug,
federal agencies skate,
industry inspectors slither
like snakes in the Basin.
I'm on my third, sipping slow,
licking salt from the rim
as I siphon the drink
through a straw, watch the level
of liquid—tequila, melting ice,
margarita mix—remain the same.

By this time, we all agree
that not much will get done
until the oil travels
around the tip of Florida,

up the east coast, washes
onto the banks of the Potomac,
rolls up the Capitol steps
and gushes right into
the halls of Congress.

Louisiana Purchase

Little white house on a corner lot
bright red porch posts, huge shade trees
and a black and white For Sale sign

in the front yard. *It'll need fixin' up*
my husband says, *should take
only a few months.* When he crawls

under the house to fix the gas leak,
pipes crumble, turn to dust in his hands.
He disappears for days, replacing

sewer lines, water pipes, emerging at night
exhausted, covered with Louisiana mud
mixed with lord knows what else.

Air conditioner, newly installed, so cold
that ceiling tiles shrivel, collapse, one tile
at a time, Celotex pieces all over the floor.

Moldy bathtub perches precariously
on rusted pipes like a boat in dry-dock, floor
beneath rotted out. He knocks down walls,

creates closet spaces, scrapes off layers
of wallpaper—thousands of petrified insects,
mouse shit, roach eggs trapped for decades, fall free

to the ground. A leaky roof uncovers
three layers of roofing—cedar, asphalt, slate—
like bandages wrapped around a wound that never heals.

New roof, windows, walls, fixtures, ceilings,
floors. *America got a better deal from Napoleon*
at three cents an acre. What exactly did we get

for our money? I ask, watching our dollars
disappear into that giant sinkhole
called repair, renovate and rebuild.

A Louisiana home, my husband answers,
where we can cook meals, invite friends, talk, read
write, relax, fight about the house, and make up.

Winter in Louisiana

Our house perches on pillars
high above the muddy earth
so it won't wash away in the floods

inviting winter wind to whistle
through the empty space beneath,
cold to seep through floorboards

the floor so cold the cats sleep atop
the washer, their soft bodies burrowed
in heaps of laundry, purring against each other

the way my body purrs
against yours on winter nights
my belly pressed against your back

my toes frozen as the hibiscus
that once filled the front yard
the grass outside brown, withered

in this soggy land where trees tumble down
in the blink of a hurricane's eye
leaving a barren landscape

with only you, sturdy as a live oak
and me, a weeping willow, moss dripping
from my fingertips, like the moss you draped

over my shoulders, *Cajun fox* you called it
when you wooed me wet like a river
to the only landscape you love.

Needing Green

I've always needed green to heal my heart
from the burnt asphalt of city sidewalks
where I prowled, city girl, until I discovered

where spirit blossoms best. When my lover
chopped down the trees in our yard, I left
our Louisiana house. The massive oak

hunkering in the middle of the lawn
with its twisted roots tunneling beneath
the house, uprooting rusty pipes—did

that dowager really have to come down?
I missed the leafy arms of the piney cedars
he thought unsightly, said the branches

would surely crash through the roof
in a hurricane. I'd rather replace tile
than chop down a tree. Then he cut away

the asparagus green barrier bushes,
jungle jade foliage hugging the side
of the house—moss, olive, teal,

leaving me exposed on that sterile street,
surrounded by neighbors' manicured
gardens, overly tended flower beds.

I wanted to worship under tea-leaf towers,
celadon umbrellas, sacred places to pray,
I wanted banana trees with bottle green leaves,

lush, tropical, jockeying for space, I wanted
clump bamboo, shooting up, multiplying,
camouflaging our wire-mesh fence, bending over

to whisper to me on my backyard stoop
where I sat, toes furled in velvety St. Augustine
grass. I wanted fern, myrtle, laurel and malachite

the color of walrus tears on a rocky shore
in Maine, where I will go now to live amidst
coastal rocks covered with barnacles and moss.

Turtles Move at the Reported Pace of Turtles

Come see, my husband says, handing me
binoculars. He's watching a turtle climb up
the ramp of the wooden turtle trap.

Usually it's herons, ducks, cottonmouths—
creatures that fly or slither away
before I can focus, but this time no rush.

I adjust—a shell comes into focus, a neck
stretches, a pea-sized head slowly cranes
left to right. One stunted bowleg at a time

moves up the ramp, flails, finds its footing
moves back, then forward again. Below
five turtles already trapped claw

at wooden walls, tumble over one another,
trying to climb out. Like the turtle
in the Balinese creation myth, this one too

seems to carry the weight of the world
on its back. I pity these shell dwellers but
my husband says they disturb the pond ecology—

he built this trap to bring them to the bayou
where they'll live undisturbed.
An hour slides by, the sun wanes, I'm tired

but can't look away for fear of missing
the climactic moment—the turtle reaches the top
the boards tilt open, the tumble into the trap.

And my friends up north wonder what I do
down here for entertainment without museums
Broadway shows, galleries I left behind.

IV

Unmoored

Deep in my body my scarlet heart floats
tries to find its moorings as it traverses time
between two lands, too many loves left behind.

My body drifts, a shadow in its own wake,
doesn't know where to drop anchor, where
to plant its misshapen feet. Down south

it abides in a cathedral space, holy shoulders
of an open loft, no place to hide, to seek itself.
It craves a container, safe haven to expand,

fill words on an empty page. Here, in the over-
heated south even the cat claims my space, wakes me
with whiskers tickling my face, whispers *move over*.

Here, my heart plays Cajun fiddle, dances, drinks,
parties day into night, or rests on the deck gazing
at turtles, carp inhaling green streamers of pond grass.

Up in the snow-blanketed north, my heart is a cello
playing solo, deep and resonant. Family and friends
provide occasional stringed accompaniment. There

I sit alone on my suede sofa, surrounded by corners
of rooms that contain me. There, I sleep alone, rise alone,
and my heart shrivels with longing for the other

but expands with the blessing of privacy. Where
to moor my heart, which once loved to wander, now aches
for one anchor to weather the waves of old age.

Snow White Sees the Mirror

Is that a strand of gray you see?
    What does the mirror say, if not that you are

not what you seem to be, not what
    you think? You are vapor

poured into a vase, delivered
    in smoke and sharp angles, a wolf

in bear's skin, howling and hairy
    sharp-mouthed, tongue-tied

to another face in the distance,
    a leopard king, a goat. Which animal

within you will appear without skin,
    without a furnace to contain your rage?

Where is the mantle to keep your calm?
    Where is your crown?

Sinking

I throw away my hair dye—
my husband has been after me for years,

thinks gray hair and wrinkles are sexy
but he's from Louisiana where women age fat

and fast in the sun. I'm beginning to look
like my mother who bemoaned her folded face

for years until she gambled on a facelift
at seventy. I can picture her still

staring in the mirror, tugging at her skin.
For years I did nothing—no facials,

toners, Botox—Jergens lotion kept me smooth
as a piece of waxy fruit. Now it's all sinking—

ravines, gullies, and a computer filled
with pop-ups hawking facelifts

and wrinkle creams, trying to persuade me
that I shouldn't trust the comforts

of home-made crawfish étouffée, duck gumbo,
potatoes fried in goose fat, and a man who accepts

the erosion of all things, promises to build us
floating motorized wheelchairs to ride out

hurricanes and the rising waters in our backyard
as Louisiana, too, sinks ever deeper into the sea.

Is Your Present Condition Due to an Accident?

—Upon limping into the doctor's office and filling out forms—

My present condition is due to aging,
an accident I had hoped to avoid,
as one hopes to avoid a plane crash,
a ship sinking in a storm,
a car pinwheeling on an icy road.

It's an accident in slow motion,
a maelstrom of mysterious malfunctions—
bones shrinking, ligaments stretching
with occasional moments of excitement—
a tibial tendon snaps suddenly
while walking down a flight of stairs,
an emergency trip to the chiropractor
after a night of zydeco dancing.

Inhabiting this ancient body has become
a journey into the unknown, a voyage
in a vintage vehicle, mishandled,
overused, with too much mileage
for the size of its engine,

a broken-down car in the dead of night
in the midst of a cross-country odyssey,
no repair shop in sight,
the local mechanic asleep behind the wheel
of his own dusty adventure.

Lubricants, leg lifts, fuel injections—
no use trying to prevent

this gradual cascade of calamities.
Better to clutch one another
and brace ourselves
for the wild, downhill ride.

Decades Later I Return to Paris

A massive sculpture dominates
Place Lucien Herr behind the Sorbonne
where I rest on a wooden bench.

In the powerful stone blocks
of rearing horse and rider, I recognize
the work of my old lover.

I return to my hotel, look him up,
dial his number, say my name.
Silence. *Hola chica,*

he finally says, *Donde estas?*
I answer, *En Paris.* He responds, *Come visit.*
I grab a taxi to his place. He opens

the door to his courtyard, with his half-
cynical, half-welcoming smile. Gray streaks
his dark hair, cropped short now.

We sit together at a wrought iron table
in stunned delight soaking up
the sight of one another. His atelier

overflows with rounded madonnas
carved in ecstatic repose, alongside
pieces of scrap metal welded together

on primitive hunks of wood. I meet
his young fiancée, pregnant with his child,
as I had been at her age, and marvel

at her happiness, feel a need to beg forgiveness
for a deed done long ago he knew nothing
about. By an act of grace, I hold back.

Five years later I come across
his bio, his date of birth followed
by a date of death and a chasm opens

deep within, as if I had again lost
the child carved in stone I'd carried
inside me all these years.

Gardening in the Dark

Mornings, I snip off flowers rusted round the edges, fasten the flower bodies
      in my hair. Afternoons I pour them a drink of rainwater,

watch the wilted petals unfurl, then peer into each flower's fuzzy center,
      examine each new bud about to open, as if searching

for god. Will essence of flower yield a message—where to meet my sister
      after she's gone? Where do skeptical souls like ours meet?

We've lived as proud heretics, no rabbis, no priests to guide us,
      no one tell us where to get off the train as it chugs

into the afterlife, like Jews to Treblinka, ashes to ashes the earth swallows,
      do we just disappear into the dark? I wish

I could conceive a heavenly architecture, is it too late?
      I dreamt once that a winged creature—an angel maybe—

led us to a train. My sister and I got on. At the first stop
      our parents appeared on the platform,

their bodies braided in death, tilted towards the tracks.
      How did they know we were coming?

I'll visit my sister tomorrow—we'll meet in her garden
      where she rests, weary, on a wicker chair, waiting.

Here, Now

My sister now lives
in a zone between life and death—
the family too is in limbo,
that classy motel,
as my Catholic friend calls it,
where you wait. But we Jews
know no such place.

My sister sleeps, wakes, dozes.
Most days she's too tired to rise
from the loveseat, opened now
into a lumpy bed, surrounded by clutter—
books, newspapers, magazines, clippings.
A magnificent samovar sits on the mantel,
reminder of our parents' lifetime romance
with Soviet Russia, their communist past.

On good days she sits upright
in a leather chair with wide wooden arms
to cradle a cup of tea, a biscuit—
arms that help her to rise, if
she has strength to haul herself up.

Bruises on her face fade slowly
from a fall face down on the slate
patio. The stray cats stood still
and stared. The pansies trembled
as she tumbled to the ground.

Some days she focuses on
what she wants to eat. Now
it's cheese—brie, blue, gouda. Now
an urge for chocolate brownies.
Her husband goes in search of

what will nourish her wasted
limbs, her bloated belly.

The doctor suggests hospice.
Her husband wavers, won't
go there. He wants one more
day, one more hour. He's hoarding
her. We're all hoarding her.

She's direct now, impatient if I grumble
about Mom and Dad. *They meant well*
she says, *and I loved them but they're gone,
and it's too late to change who we are.*

Maybe it's easier for those of us
with a future to revisit the past.
Tears fall—hers, then mine.
She understands something I don't yet.

Now she needs to lie down. She asks
her husband to bring in *those pink peonies
and blue irises. Put some in a vase,
and wrap some up in wet paper towels
for my sister to take home.*

At the Wake of My Ex-Husband's Third Wife

—For Cathy—

She snatched him from the jaws
of our divorce, only slightly mangled
but on the mend, an established doctor,

dry now, in demand. I was impressed
by how she managed their life, brought order
to chaos, planned ahead, made her way his—

tickets to Broadway, trips to Paris, Prague,
Tiffany trinkets, leather sofas, an Audi,
a Saab, while back in the day he refused

to pay to have our rusted-out Dodge re-painted,
its dented fenders fixed. *You were younger,*
she said, *didn't know how to fight*

for your rights. I study her photo display—
head wrapped in a turban, she grins into
the camera, voracious teeth gleaming,

her smile almost a shriek, mingling joy
with rage, as if there was not enough time
to devour all life's offerings. Gone now,

that ordered life, undone by her body
unleashing its secret after all those years—
a tangled mass of arteries and veins

at the base of her brain waiting, silently
waiting, bursting like a roman candle—
a bloodletting, a letting down, a letting go.

Recovery Room

Shadow figures flit before me—
  profile of a blond ponytail, a phantom
    filling a syringe, a dark-haired man,

a demon, wheeling in bodies
  strapped to beds, all of us prisoners,
    consigned to a den deep in middle earth.

Memories surface—
  high ceiling, bright lights, surgeon
    joking before he breaks into my heart,

me wanting to cry out,
  Beware, it's been broken
  before, may not mend as it should.

The story of my broken heart—
  you know it well—archaic, trite,
    the usual misuse and abuse, chords

stretched thin, a tattered valve letting blood
  spill into neighboring chambers, the heart
    pumping too hard, a dangerous dance of stop

and go. Cut, stitch, clamp
  with a silver ring. Damage repaired,
    they ferry me back, a gurney over the river Styx,

to an underground cave where bodies
  lie moaning in a tangle of tubes, beeps,
    blinking lights. Kindly gnomes rush to and fro,

medicating pain, monitoring
  heartbeats as I lie swaddled, nursing
    from tubes, a newborn, awaiting the sunlight.

Sex After Seventy-Nine

I imagine will happen from time
to time, aging neurons ignited

by random memories, a sultry song
and one of us remembers it's something

we used to adore—provided
we retain the thought

for as long as it takes to catch the eye
of a partner wandering the perimeter

of waking moments. By the time
we both arrive in the bedroom

let's hope we recall why
we are there and what appendages

go where. It would be wise
to keep the nightstand stocked

with creams, oils and mechanical
devices so as not to succumb to surprise

or despair should body parts not rise
to the occasion. Magazines, videos, pre-coital

naps may be considered foreplay
in this new terrain of terminally ancient

but willing to give it a try before
ceding to the god of indifference

and succumbing to the rapture
of sleep.

Signifiers

I fall face down on concrete
en route from a book fair, treasures
in hand, a day of grace until I stumble,

propelled through air thinking,
"I'm too old for this shit." But
that's what old people do—we fall.

As I tumble to the ground, I wonder
what will break—knee, hand, elbow,
face—the pavement greets them all.

My radius cracks, my middle finger
slips from its socket, swells so my ring
has to be cut off for X-rays—

turquoise and silver encircling
my finger for forty years, marking
the birth of my son. Talisman lost,

my finger wags naked in the world.
We were bound together, time
to cut him loose. And if the ring stays off,

who will fill the void?
Meanwhile I limp, arm in a sling,
middle finger pointing skywards.

Carapace

There's a finality to it, the body
on a slab, white sheet up to her chin,
the waxy sheen of her face, the lips
shriveled, looking as if they'd been stitched
together, the eyes shut, sewed down.

Impossible to mistake my sister's body
for living, the way some bodies look
before burial—dressed, combed, powdered,
as if they might open their eyes and greet you.

I remember when our mother
came home from the hospital, cradling
a bundle wrapped to the chin
in white blankets—only a tiny face
peeked out. *This is your sister,* she said.

And I remember how a year later,
my sister toddled over to me, a baby
wearing only a diaper, as I sat
at my little table in the kitchen
putting together a puzzle. She held out
a puzzle piece that had dropped on the floor.

Pees pugga, Baba—her name for me—
I think how it started back then, how
through the years she helped me put together
the jumbled puzzle pieces of my life.

There's a finality to it, the shock
of her lifeless body. My heart constricts
then opens wide. This is an empty shell,
a ravaged carapace, not my sister. I wonder
where she's gone.

Afterlife

I've never believed in one. Nor did
my sister, which made it difficult
to decide where we would meet.
So there's no explanation as to why,

a week after she died, I looked up,
and saw her floating above me, reclining
on her side, her head propped on one arm
looking as she did twenty years ago

before age and illness ransacked
her body. She was relaxed and smiling,
dressed as usual in jeans, a sweater,
golden-brown hair framing her face.

I had been dancing to music, waving my arms
in the air. When our eyes met, she leaned over
and extended her arm, reaching down as if
to grasp my hand. Not to pull me up to her,

nor for me to pull her to the earth,
but just to comfort me, letting me know
she was at peace and would be waiting
whenever I was ready to join her

What Will You Do?

with the waning stretch of life you have left,
where you find yourself awakened,

an aging Snow White kissed
by remorse and an itch for more,

amid these years that swiftly stream
that buzz like bees in heat—*do me, do me.*

Will you write your political poems, read
those books on your shelf, march in protests,

cheer at rallies, dance the Argentine tango,
play Bach on the piano, learn the blues?

So many deeds left undone. Will you drown, do
a dead-woman's float or defy the current?

These looming, late-blooming years
both creep and sprint, they moan

and howl with want, the dark a dirge
you know is there but cannot see or hear.

So you go forward, your creaky frame
grown askew, wondering too, are you still

beloved? True your face droops, your skin pools
like nylons over bony knees, your muscles melt,

but your mind remains a spinning top, shining
into dark corners, squinting in bright light,

grows daily more demanding. You rise
chanting, *Is there time, is there time?*

Acknowledgments

Many thanks to the editors of the publications in which these poems first appeared, sometimes in earlier versions.

Learning to Love Louisiana, (Yellow Flag Press): "Meeting Leo" as "Collision: A Lovesong," "Watching Him Peel an Onion," "Making Love with a Southern Boy," "Road Widow," "Hurricane Lily Wilts to a Category Two," "Mistaken and Forsaken," "How to Visit Cajun Country," as "Arrival" "He Visits Me," "Living Alone," "Deciding to Marry," "Learning to Love Louisiana," "Winter in Louisiana."

Louisiana Purchase, (Yellow Flag Press): "Tar Beach," "Dyckman and Broadway," "Writing on the Wall," "Married to My House" "Needing Green," "Repetition Compulsion," "Drinking Margaritas and Talking about the Oil Spill"

Duet—Poet & Photographer, (Yellow Flag Press): "Madame Bellefleur," "Catechism," "The Road Widow"

About Place: "Needing Green"

Atlanta Review: "Is Your Present Condition Due to an Accident?"

Calyx: "Uncle Hershey" and "Winter in Louisiana"

Cadillac Ciccatrix: "Autumn in Paris" as "Summer in Paris"

The Examined Life: "Recovery Room"

Gyroscope: "Signifiers"

Louisiana Literature: "What Shape Awaits in the Seed of You?"

Louisiana Review: "Hurricane Lily Wilts to A Category Two"

Naugatuck River Review: "Bloodlines" as "Bloodlines—A Family Crapshoot," and "Still a Spinster at Twenty-Seven"

Mocking Heart Review: "My Mother's Dreams" and "What Will You Do?"

Nelle: "Sinking"

Passager, Poetry Contest, Honorable Mention: "At the Wake of My Ex-Husband's Third Wife"

PANK, "Many Mysteries" as "What's Said One Day Is Reversed the Next"

Rattle: "Living Alone"

Red Wheelbarrow: "Deciding to Marry"

Rogue Agent: "Internship—Pittsburgh, 1979"

Sanskrit: "Meeting Leo," as "Collision–A Lovesong"

Southern Poetry Anthology, Vol IV: "He Visits Me," and "Learning to Love Louisiana"

Spillway: "Phantom Child"

The Poets Speak, Greenburg Competition: "Married to My House"

A Twist in Time: "Snow White Sees the Mirror"

Valley Voices: "Turtles Move at the Reported Pace of Turtles," and "Unmoored"

Vision Verse: "The Sofa of my Dreams" as "Ticking"

Westchester Review: "Come In"

Westview: "The Road Widow"

Wisconsin Review: "Learning to Love Louisiana"

Deepest gratitude to my fellow writers and friends who encouraged me, especially to Anne Graue, who helped me put this manuscript together, and to Ellen Devlin, Karen Gershowitz, Geri Kaplan. Mara Mills, and Judy Rabinor who critiqued many versions of these poems with patience, insight, and good humor.

I am indebted to the Hudson Valley Writers Center where I learned to write poetry, and to its talented and supportive teachers and writing community for their wise counsel and guidance.

Many thanks to my Baton Rouge poetry group; y'all make writing so much fun. Who else can spend twenty minutes on a comma and laugh about it!

Special thanks in memory of my dear friend Janet Nehrbass who encouraged me to write many of the Louisiana poems that fill my books.

Immense appreciation to my family, especially to my son, Justin, for his generosity and steadfast acceptance of his off-beat mom, and to my sister Jane whose friendship and unconditional love I miss every day. To my granddaughter Sunflower who has begun their own writing life at an early age—they are an inspiration.

Loving thanks to my husband Leo Touchet who brought me to Louisiana, this foreign land of grace and grit (and bad hair days). He ignites the writing spark buried within me and challenges me to share my poetry with the world.

Finally, huge thanks and gratitude to Texas Review Press and in particular to J. Bruce Fuller, generous editor and supporter of my writing. I could not have taken this journey without him.

About the Author

ELIZABETH BURK is a psychologist, a native New Yorker who divides her time between family in New York and a home and husband in southwest Louisiana. She is the author of three previous collections, *Learning to Love Louisiana, Louisiana Purchase,* and *Duet: Poet & Photographer,* a collaboration with her husband, Leo Touchet. Her poems, prose pieces, and reviews have been published in numerous journals and anthologies, including *Atlanta Review, Calyx, Rattle, Southern Poetry Anthology, Louisiana Literature, Passager, Pithead Chapel, PANK, Rogue Agent,* and *ONE ART: A Journal of Poetry.*

The Sabine Series in Literature

Series Editor: J. Bruce Fuller

The Sabine Series in Literature highlights work by authors born in or working in Eastern Texas and/or Louisiana. There are no thematic restrictions; TRP seeks the best writing possible by authors from this unique region of the American South.

BOOKS IN THIS SERIES:

Cody Smith, *Gulf*

David Armand, *The Lord's Acre*

Ron Rozelle, *Leaving the Country of Sin*

Collier Brown, *Scrap Bones*

Esteban Rodríguez, *Lotería*

Elizabeth Burk, *Unmoored*

Cliff Hudder, *Sallowsfield*